The Beauty Palace

Copyright © 2013 by Sue Young

THE BEAUTY PALACE

By Sue Young

Characters

CHRISTINE Beautician
PAMELA Beautician
ROSE Customer
CONNIE Customer
SHERRY Customer
DEVIANT Dodgy Customer
BRUTUS Pamela's Boyfriend
ROGER Christine's Boyfriend
COLIN Salesman/ Inventor

SYNOPSIS

The Beauty Palace is a busy salon run by Christine and Pamela. It is a place where customers can relax, gossip and sort out their complicated love lives. Thrown into the mix is Colin, a local inventor of beauty products, who experiments on the salon's customers, often with disastrous results.

Authors Note

Only one set is needed for the entire play, there are no scene changes. The set should be designed to look like a beauty salon. This play, was performed as a double bill with 'Green Bananas' in 2013 with the Lancastrian Players, and along with it, broke the record for highest takings in the history of the company.

Running Time (approx) : 1 hour

SCENE 1

(ENTER CHRISTINE AND PAMELA)

PAMELA: Monday morning. 9 o'clock. My favourite time of the week.

CHRISTINE: Really? You don't mean that?

PAMELA: I like coming to work.

CHRISTINE: Well, you know me, I love my weekends, but this ones been hell.

PAMELA: Really? Nothing to do with Roger I hope.

CHRISTINE: No. It was those builders again, started up right under my bedroom window, first thing.

PAMELA: Lucky you.

CHRISTINE: You don't know what it was like. All that drilling.

PAMELA: Oh, that reminds me, Brutus stayed the weekend.

CHRISTINE: (PAUSE) Isn't he that Greek guy you've been seeing?

PAMELA: Yes.

CHRISTINE: Like him do you?

PAMELA: Oh yes. (PAUSE) But he's a bit hairy.

CHRISTINE: Pam, that's too much information.

PAMELA: What I meant to say was, I've been trying to get him to come in for a wax.

CHRISTINE:How bad is it?

PAMELA: Werewolf proportions.

CHRISTINE: I don't know how you stand it.

PAMELA: Oh it's okay. It's like cuddling up to a warm welcome mat.

Also, he's double sided.

CHRISTINE: What's that?

PAMELA: Hair on both sides. I could go into detail.

CHRISTINE: Don't please. It's too early.

PAMELA: So, how is Roger ?

CHRISTINE: He's fine.

PAMELA: He doesn't have a hairy problem.

CHRISTINE: No he doesn't. Wait, how would you know that ?

PAMELA: I did a body wrap on him last week.

CHRISTINE: What? He came in here? Where was I?

PAMELA: He did come to see you but you were shopping that afternoon. So I did him.

CHRISTINE: I hope you averted your eyes.

PAMELA: Of course. I was very professional. Although...

CHRISTINE: Yes?

PAMELA: He does have nice legs.

CHRISTINE: You shouldn't have been down that end. (PAMELA LOOKS SHEEPISH) Now, check list...hot rollers, curling tongs, straighteners.

PAMELA : Oh yes, on standby.

CHRISTINE: Facials?

PAMELA: Yes, ready and waiting for a face. Those new Lavender and Jasmine packs came in the other day. They're scrumptious.

CHRISTINE: Oh good. How are we doing for shampoo, conditioner and hair dye?

PAMELA: A little low on stock but we can cope.

CHRISTINE: Cleanser, toner, moisturiser and creams?

PAMELA: All present and correct.

CHRISTINE: And finally wax strips, body masks and wraps?

PAMELA: I'm on top of that. There are two dozen of each in the wet room.

CHRISTINE: So, who's up first ?

PAMELA: Let me look in the book. Er... nine o'clock...oh no...

CHRISTINE: What's up?

PAMELA: Rose is booked in for nine-o-five.

CHRISTINE: Five past nine? Why did you book her in for that time?

PAMELA: She's going to a wedding at one?

CHRISTINE: A wedding on Monday afternoon?

PAMELA: She sits at the back of the church. She likes to see what the bride is wearing.

CHRISTINE: We haven't even got the kettle on. I'm not in the mood for all the idle gossip and senseless chatter.

PAMELA: But this place was built on idle gossip and senseless chatter.

SCENE 2

CHRISTINE: (QUIETLY) Speak of the devil. (ENTER ROSE) Good Morning Rose.

ROSE: (SWEETLY): Hello Pamela. (COLDLY): Any chance of a cup of tea Christine? (CHRISTINE EXITS TO MAKE SOME TEA). What's up with her ? She's a bit of a sour puss this morning.

PAMELA: She's got builders outside her bedroom window. She's tired.

ROSE: Mrs. Farley from next door said Christine is going out with her son Roger. You know Roger ?

PAMELA: Only without his clothes and covered in a Honey and Juniper body wrap.

ROSE: Well anyway, I'm not sure I like her manner. She keeps giving me daggers.

PAMELA : That might be because you keep sending her out to make tea. (ENTER CHRISTINE)

CHRISTINE: I made coffee. I thought we could all do with it. Pamela... (HANDS COFFEE TO PAMELA).

PAMELA: Thanks.

ROSE: What about me? (CHRISTINE HANDS COFFEE TO ROSE). Where are the biscuits?

(CHRISTINE GETS A PLATE OF BISCUITS FOR ROSE).

CHRISTINE:(SARCASTICALLY): Thank you Christine. Oh, no, it was no trouble at all.

PAMELA: So how are you today Rose?

ROSE: Feet playing up.

PAMELA: You need to soak them in hot water. We have a very nice peppermint foot soak.

ROSE: Okay, I'll go for that.

PAMELA: Anything else? What would you like me to do for this wedding?

ROSE: It's one of those shotgun ones, so nothing too fancy.

PAMELA: How about a lemon and green tea facial ?

ROSE: That sounds nice. Has he been in today?

CHRISTINE: Who?

ROSE: No-one you should be concerned about.

PAMELA: She's talking about Colin.

ROSE: I was hoping to see him today.

PAMELA: He was in on Friday.

CHRISTINE: He's never away from here.

PAMELA: You are a bit obsessed Rose.

ROSE: Has he invented it yet?

PAMELA: Since Friday, no.

CHRISTINE: Invented what?

PAMELA: You know...

ROSE: It.

CHRISTINE: Oh I remember now, the face cream.

ROSE: No, it's a wonder cream and it's going to change the world. He's an inventor.

CHRISTINE: He's not an inventor. He's a salesman.

ROSE: He invents things doesn't he? That makes him an inventor.

PAMELA: Keep still Rose, or I'll have this all over your hair. Now in a short while, this face pack will tighten and you won't be able to talk.

(CHRISTINE AND PAMELA EXCHANGE A LOOK)

ROSE: Oh, I'm quite happy with being quiet. In fact, Mrs. Brown from the bakery said she's never known a quieter person than me. That's why it takes her ages to serve me. Oh yes, I can feel it start to tighten now.

(ROSE CLOSES HER EYES AND APPEARS TO NOD OFF, CHRISTINE BECKONS PAMELA TO HER. THEY SIT DOWN AND RELAX FOR A MOMENT)

SCENE 3

(ENTER COLIN WITH A SUITCASE)

COLIN: I've got it ! (EVERYONE IS STARTLED. ROSE WAKES UP). I've got it...and it's going to be huge. I am. I mean...this is....going to be... (GETS A BIT BREATHLESS)

CHRISTINE: You're getting too excited Colin.

PAMELA: Come on, sit down. Catch your breath.

COLIN: No thank you, I'd rather stand.

ROSE: So you've invented it then? The face cream?

COLIN: It's not just any face cream Rose. It's a cream that's going to change the world, as we know it. It is the face cream that will make every lady kneel at my feet and even some who aren't ladies. It is the face cream that will put me on the map.

CHRISTINE: What map is that?

COLIN: Er...well...the map of being the inventor of the miracle face cream. This will make botox look like...like something you buy in the pound shop.

CHRISTINE: 9.20 a.m Monday Morning and already a life changing event.

COLIN: Oh that reminds me. (HE TAKES OUT A WILTING BUNCH OF FLOWERS FROM HIS SUITCASE AND GIVES THEM TO CHRISTINE) For you.

CHRISTINE: Oh thank you Colin. That's very sweet. I'll put them in some water.

COLIN: Now where was I. Oh yes, form an orderly queue ladies please.

ROSE: I'm first.

PAMELA: You do realise we're just guinea pigs.

ROSE: I don't mind.

COLIN: It might tingle a bit.

ROSE: Just put it on.

(HE PUTS THE FACE CREAM ON PAMELA, CHRISTINE AND ROSE)

COLIN: Okay. Feel anything?

ROSE: No.

PAMELA: Not yet.

CHRISTINE: How long will we have to wait ? We have two 9.30 appointments coming up.

PAMELA: It is tingling a bit.

CHRISTINE: Oh yes, very warming. It's quite nice actually.

ROSE: I don't feel anything.

PAMELA: Oh. It's getting uncomfortably warm now.

CHRISTINE : Yes, it's starting to burn.

ROSE: I don't feel anything.

PAMELA: Oh ! Ow ! Ow!

CHRISTINE: Ahhhhh !

(BOTH CHRISTINE AND PAMELA EXIT QUCKLY TO WASH OFF THE CREAM)

COLIN: Was it the shark oil? Could it have been the whale vomit? Maybe I put in too much chilli powder.

(SOUNDS OF RELIEF FROM BACKSTAGE AS THE CREAM IS

WASHED OFF)

ROSE: I don't feel anything.

COLIN: Maybe you should wash it off Rose, just to be on the safe side.

(HE LEADS HER AWAY)

ROSE: Did you get it wrong Colin ?

COLIN: I think I did. It could have been the fermented sea kelp, the amino acids, maybe something to do with the peptides.

ROSE:Never mind Colin. There's always next time.

COLIN: Yes. Let's get that washed off before it takes half your face off.

(EXIT COLIN AND ROSE)

SCENE 4

(ENTER SHERRY)

SHERRY: Where is everyone? Oh well, I'll just sit here. Oh coffee...
(DRINKS SOME COFFEE)
(ENTER CONNIE, DRESSED AS THE QUEEN) Oh, hello Connie.

CONNIE: Good Morning. Where are my subjects today?

SHERRY: Oh wait, er...let me guess...who are you today? (LOOKS HER UP AND DOWN)

CONNIE: I usually get a curtsey. Good job my royal body guards aren't here. They would have something to say about that.

SHERRY: Oh. You're the Queen.(SHERRY COURTSEYS IN FRONT OF CONNIE) Okay. Happy now?

CONNIE: Please address me as your majesty.

SHERRY: Sorry, your majesty. Wonder where Christine and Pamela are ?

CONNIE: That's what I just said.

SHERRY: You can't very well run a beauty parlour without a beautician now can you?

CONNIE: You can't keep someone like me waiting for too long. It's simply not done.

SHERRY: Just sit down Connie.

CONNIE: Where does one sit?

SHERRY: There, your majesty.

CONNIE: I'm to be addressed as Ma' am, after the initial address of your majesty.

SHERRY: Make up your mind.

CONNIE: And then, your majesty again, upon leaving.

SHERRY: Whatever.

CONNIE: It is customary for the seat to be wiped down lightly before I sit, so as not to soil my rear...dress area.

(SHERRY SPITS ON HER HAND AND WIPES THE SEAT) I think I'll stand.

SHERRY: Suit yourself. You should get some of this nail polish. Catches the attention of all the men, even in a dark nightclub. Sends them wild.

CONNIE: I don't know. Looks rather common to me.

SHERRY: Colin sold it to me last week.

CONNIE: Who?

SHERRY: You know Colin, the bloke who sells Christine and Pamela shampoo and stuff.

CONNIE: Are men even allowed in here?

SHERRY: Of course they are Connie. You've seen men come in before. Oh, I forgot. You've led a sheltered life, you're the Queen. This is a unisex salon.

CONNIE: Unisex ? One thinks that sounds a bit dodgy.

SHERRY: It just means men and women can come in and have beauty treatments.

CONNIE: Why would men want beauty treatments?

SHERRY: It's all the rage now. They're even starting to smell better than us. They call them metrosexuals.

CONNIE: Metro what? I mean, could you please repeat that, one did not quite catch it ?

SHERRY: You know men who pamper and preen themselves. We get a few in now and again. They just don't seem to be here when you're here.

(ENTER COLIN)

CONNIE: Oh, but here's one now.

SHERRY: A man ? Oh, that's just Colin.

COLIN: Good morning ladies.

SHERRY: Less of the ladies. We're women. Strong, sexy women.

COLIN: Oh er...yes.

SHERRY: Bow to the queen Colin. (COLIN LOOKS AROUND) The queen. She's right there.

COLIN: But it's just Connie.

SHERRY: Just do it. (COLIN BOWS DEEPLY) Do you have any more of that nail polish Colin?

COLIN: Which one?

SHERRY: It's called chameleon.

COLIN: Ah yes, chameleon. It's a good seller. (THEY EXCHANGE MONEY AND GOODS)

Where is everybody ? Is Christine about?

SCENE 5

(ENTER CHRISTINE AND PAMELA)

SHERRY: Where have you been ? What's up with your faces?

CHRISTINE: It's Colin's latest disaster and I'm surprised he's got the gall to show his face round here again.

COLIN: I came to apologise.

CHRISTINE: Oh more flowers. Thank you Colin.

PAMELA: But what about our faces?

SHERRY: What did you do to them?

PAMELA: He gave us a sample of his face cream. His miracle cream.

SHERRY: Oh those creams never work. No offence Colin.

COLIN: None taken.

PAMELA: Hello Connie. Why are you dressed like that?

CONNIE: My clothes were made for me by the Queens Tailors. My tailors, I mean. I am dressed in the manner becoming to the Queen.

SHERRY: You'd better curtsey or her royal aides will be after you.

(PAMELA AND CHRISTINE CURTSEY)

CONNIE It is an education to experience the environment of the common working man. To smell the sweat and toil of his livelihood. It is most humbling.

(ENTER ROSE)

PAMELA: Oh Rose, how's your face after yesterday?

ROSE: It's fine. It didn't burn at all. You two make such a fuss.

CHRISTINE: Excuse me, Rose, but it was like having a hundred chilli peppers on our skin.

ROSE: A hundred ? Oh you do exaggerate Christine. Pamela, what about that foot bath ?

CHRISTINE: Look at our faces Rose. Hey, wait a minute, why isn't your face red?

ROSE: I told you it didn't bother me. You must have had an abnormal reaction to it. There was probably nothing wrong with the cream at all. Poor Colin. His reputation has been sullied for nothing.

CHRISTINE: His reputation has not be sullied for nothing. It has been sullied for a very good reason.

ROSE: I don't know what you're complaining about, a bit of red is good for the face. You'll save money on rouge. Now shove up. You're in my seat.

SHERRY: Last time I looked it didn't have your name on it.

ROSE: Move. (ROSE MAKES SHERRY MOVE UP)

PAMELA: Well, it doesn't feel too bad now. We haven't been disfigured for life. We'll live. So let's all chill out and have some nice relaxing beauty treatments.   Now, ladies, sorry to keep you waiting. What will it be ?

ROSE: I'm having a foot bath remember ?

SHERRY: Nails.

PAMELA: You have lovely hands Sherry. Strange nail polish though.

SHERRY: It changes colour all the time. It was great when I was out clubbing last night.

PAMELA: What's it called?

SHERRY: Chameleon, but it's all chipped off so I need a manicure. I'm going out again   tonight. It's a two hour happy hour at my local.

CONNIE: One's feet are sore standing up like this.

CHRISTINE: Well, sit down.

SHERRY: The chairs are too filthy for her majesty.

CHRISTINE: I'll get you a handkerchief. Don't worry, it's clean.
(PLACES HANKERCHEIF ON CHAIR)

CONNIE: Now that's what I call manners but I will decline your kind offer and return to Buckingham Palace. The corgi's need feeding...and so does Philip.

PAMELA: This is a palace Connie.

CONNIE: Yes but this is just the beauty palace. There is a big difference. Good day to you all. You were all very entertaining.

CHRISTINE: Bye Connie. I mean your majesty. (CHRISTINE CURTSEYS)

PAMELA: Stop that.

(EXIT CONNIE)

She's bonkers.

CHRISTINE: She always wanted to be an actor but alas never got a chance.

ROSE: She's just lonely, that's all.

SCENE 6

(ENTER DEVIANT)

DEVIANT: I'd like a full body massage please.

CHRISTINE: What?

(DEVIANT STARTS WINKING AT CHRISTINE IN AN EXAGERATTED MANNER)

CHRISTINE: What's up with your eye?

DEVIANT: Can I have a full body massage. (MORE EXAGERATTED WINKING)

CHRISTINE: Oh, we're not that kind of salon. Get out of here, you dirty old man.

(EXIT **DEVIANT**)

ROSE: When am I going to get this foot bath?

PAMELA: Sorry Rose. I'll be with you in a moment.

COLIN: I've got some nice shampoo and conditioner. Makes your hair nice and   shiny.

PAMELA: Did you invent it?

COLIN: No. These are wholesale.

CHRISTINE: In that case we'll have six bottles of shampoo and six of the conditioner.

PAMELA: Let's have a look. Oh, this is the good stuff.

COLIN: And at a special price ladies.

CHRISTINE: Why didn't you tell us about it before ?

COLIN: I was distracted by the face cream.

CHRISTINE: So were we.

PAMELA: The less said about that the better.

ROSE: Never mind. No real harm done.

COLIN: People aren't buying my inventions.

CHRISTINE: Can't say I'm surprised. Just sell the wholesale and forget about the inventions.

ROSE: We love your products Colin.

CHRISTINE: Did you invent the nail polish ?

COLIN: No.

CHRISTINE: Thank God for that. You'd have no nails left Sherry.

SHERRY: Well, Chameleon is doing wonders for my love life. A bloke fell in love with me last night because I had it on. I'm seeing him again tonight.

CHRISTINE: I'd better make them look good then. Do you want me to reapply the nail polish after I've done the manicure ?

SHERRY: No. I don't want to overexcite him. Chameleon two nights on the run would probably kill him. Are you seeing anyone?

PAMELA: Yes, a guy called Brutus.

SHERRY: Brutus ? When did that start?

PAMELA: A couple of weekends ago.

SHERRY: What's his real name?

PAMELA: That is his real name.

SHERRY: Are you sure?

PAMELA: No, but he likes to be called Brutus and I like to call him Brutus.

SHERRY: What about you Christine? Seeing anyone nice?

ROSE: She's going out with Roger. (COLIN IS FUSSING AROUND

CHRISTINE). I said she's going out with Roger.

CHRISTINE: Colin, I'm fine, I really don't need you to hold the false nails for me.

COLIN: Well, I'll be off then. I'll bring some hair dye in next time, for all of you to try.

CHRISTINE: Did you invent it?

COLIN: Yes, I did.

CHRISTINE: Well in that case we don't want to know.

ROSE: I'll be your guinea pig Colin.

COLIN: Oh thank you Rose. See you all later. (EXIT COLIN)

ROSE: Pamela ? Foot bath !

SCENE 7

PAMELA: We need some extra towels from the back room.

(EXIT CHRISTINE)

ROSE: (GETS UP TO LOOK AT THE FLOWERS THAT COLIN BOUGHT FOR CHRISTINE) These flowers have got a tag.

PAMELA: What?

ROSE: The flowers that Colin bought for Christine. It says 'To Christine. Love From Colin'.

PAMELA: So?

ROSE: Love from Colin. Love.

PAMELA: (ENTER CHRISTINE WITH TOWELS). We need more.

(CHRISTINE DUMPS THE TOWELS AND EXITS AGAIN)

ROSE: Love.

PAMELA: Sorry?

ROSE: Does Roger know that Colin sends her flowers?

PAMELA: Who ?

ROSE: Christine.

PAMELA: No. Why?

ROSE: Maybe he should.

PAMELA: So tell me Sherry, what's this nail obsessed man like?

SHERRY: He's lovely but he follows me around like a puppy.

PAMELA: Really ?

SHERRY: Yes. He came back for coffee last night.

PAMELA: Oh, did he now?

SHERRY: He followed me into the kitchen.

PAMELA: Oh?

SHERRY: I went upstairs to the bathroom and he followed me in there.

PAMELA: Really?

SHERRY: Then, well you're never going to believe it...

PAMELA: Tell me.

SHERRY: I went into the bedroom....

PAMELA: Yes ?

SHERRY: And he followed me in there. (ENTER CHRISTINE WITH MORE TOWELS)

PAMELA: And?

SHERRY: Well, he...

CHRISTINE: Rose, I'll give you a foot bath in the wet room.

ROSE: At last ! But I want Pamela to do it.

CHRISTINE: Pam, you're needed.

PAMELA: And ?

SHERRY: Well...

CHRISTINE: Pam !

(PAMELA GROANS AND EXITS. ROSE EXITS)

SCENE 8

SHERRY: I think I'll go outside and dry my nails.

CHRISTINE: But we have a nail dryer.

SHERRY: I know but fresh air dries them quicker. (SHERRY GOES TO EXIT AND WAVES HER HANDS AROUND. ENTER BRUTUS. HE CHATS TO SHERRY AND FLIRTS WITH HER. SHE ENDS UP SLAPPING HIM. EXIT SHERRY. ENTER BRUTUS INTO SALON SCENE).

CHRISTINE: Pamela? We've got another customer.

PAMELA: (OFFSTAGE): Still doing Rose.

CHRISTINE: Well, hurry up. He looks even stranger than that other man.

BRUTUS: What a wonderful place. Women come here, get washed, beautified, creamed, polished, buffed up, perfumed, all shiny and sweet smelling and   ready for love. You are Christine, no?

CHRISTINE: Er...yes.

BRUTUS: Pamela has mentioned you, but she never told me just how beautiful you were.

CHRISTINE: I beg your pardon?

BRUTUS: (PUTS HIS ARM AROUND HER WAIST) You must be sisters. Sisters of beauty, no?

CHRISTINE: You must be Brutus.

BRUTUS: Yes, I am. (HOLDS HER CLOSER)

CHRISTINE: Get that chest away from me.

BRUTUS: I like two fillings in my sandwiches. Do you know what I mean Christine?

CHRISTINE: But...but Pam is in the wet room.

BRUTUS: She'll have to wait her turn.

CHRISTINE: No, I didn't mean that. You're her boyfriend.

BRUTUS: Oh, she is a very beautiful woman. She knows I love her very much.

CHRISTINE: Please take your hands off me. That thing is making me ticklish.

BRUTUS: Chest hair is manly.

(ENTER ROSE AND PAMELA)

PAMELA: Brutus.

BRUTUS: Pamela. Oh my beautiful Pamela. It is so lovely to see you at work. Very sexy uniforms! (HE PUTS HIS ARM AROUND PAMELA)

(ENTER SHERRY)

SHERRY: That man just pinched my bottom and a bit more besides. I was helpless because of my nails. Pam, please don't tell me this is Brutus?

PAMELA: Yes it is.

BRUTUS: Hi baby.

SHERRY: I make the first move mister, no-one else. Keep your medallion to yourself in future.

(EXIT SHERRY)

PAMELA: What's up Christine? You look a bit flustered.

CHRISTINE: Well, I don't want to tell tales but...his hands...were...everywhere.

PAMELA: Oh yes, I know, he likes to flirt.

BRUTUS: I'm sorry baby. I can't help myself. I just have to flirt with beautiful women. It's in my genes.

CHRISTINE:That's the problem.

PAMELA: Why are you here Brutus ?

BRUTUS: To tear you away from your life of drudgery. To take you to lunch, a long leisurely lunch with a siesta afterwards.

CHRISTINE: Isn't that the Spanish?

PAMELA: I can't Brutus. Can't you see how busy we are?

BRUTUS: I'm sure Christine will be able to cope.

PAMELA: As much as I want to, I can't. But I'll see you tonight.

BRUTUS: Ah, baby. You have disappointed me. You will have to make it up to me tonight. And who is this lovely vision ?

ROSE: Come near me and I'll throttle you with that necklace.

BRUTUS: It is not a necklace. My grand papa used to wear this. It's a love symbol, a heirloom passed down through the generations. Pamela, it will break my heart to leave you now but I will see you tonight my little snuggle wuggle bunnykin.

ROSE: Little snuggle wuggle bunnykin ?

PAMELA: See you tonight, my boggle woggle honey toes.

BRUTUS: Not before I see you first, my schmookey pookie sugar pop.

PAMELA: Bye, my lickle wickle boo boo bear.

CHRISTINE: Just go.

(EXIT BRUTUS)

SCENE 9

CHRISTINE: Thank God I've got Roger.

PAMELA: What's that supposed to mean?

CHRISTINE: Nothing. Well...

PAMELA: Well what...

CHRISTINE: You have to admit he's a bit full on. A bit too much.

(ENTER DEVIANT. THIS TIME IN DISGUISE)

DEVIANT: I'll have a full Swedish body massage please.

CHRISTINE: Talk about too much.

PAMELA: We've already told you we don't do that.

DEVIANT: No, it's not me. I mean I'm not that first guy that came in the other day

asking for a massage.

CHRISTINE: Well, for the last time, we don't do massage.

DEVIANT: Not even Swedish.

CHRISTINE: Not in any language.

DEVIANT: It says in your brochure that you do massage.

CHRISTINE: That's head massage. We also do foot.

DEVIANT: Definitely no full body Swedish?

CHRISTINE: No.

PAMELA: Although we do body masks and wraps. They do include a bit of massage.

CHRISTINE: Don't encourage him Pamela.

PAMELA: Why exactly don't we have massage as a stand alone? It calms the body after the stimulation of exfoliation.

SCENE 10

(ENTER COLIN)

COLIN: I've got it !

(EVERYONE GROANS)

CHRISTINE: What have you got Colin?

COLIN: Ah, this time it's a hair dye.

PAMELA: Did you invent it?

COLIN: Yes. Would anyone like to try it?

(EVERYONE EXITS APART FROM ROSE)

ROSE: Colin. You've frightened everyone away.

COLIN: I didn't mean to.

ROSE: I'll try the hair dye Colin.

COLIN: Okay. You can come back everyone. Rose is going to try my hair dye.

(ENTER PAM, ENTER CHRISTINE. ENTER DEVIANT)

CHRISTINE: No, not you. Shoo !

(EXIT DEVIANT)

(ENTER CONNIE)

PAMELA: Hello Connie. You've missed all the fun.

CONNIE: Vogue. Strike a pose.

CHRISTINE: Who are you today?

CONNIE: I'm an icon, a legend in my own lifetime. In fact, I've heard people say that I'm a bit of a cult.

COLIN: Would you like to try my hair dye?

CONNIE: What colour is it?

COLIN: It's a rich chestnut brown.

CONNIE: No. I can't try your hair dye Colin. I'm blonde as you can see and I have to stay blonde. I'm in the middle of my Blonde Ambition Tour.

CHRISTINE: Oh. I thought it was your Vogue Tour.

PAMELA: Is she...still playing the queen?

CHRISTINE: No, well, yes in a way. She's the Queen Of Pop.

ROSE: Come on Colin. Let's go into the wet room to dye my hair.

(EXIT COLIN. EXIT ROSE)

CONNIE: I'm a diva and as a diva I think I need a massage.

CHRISTINE: Oh, don't you start.

PAMELA: Come on, I'll give you a body mask.

CONNIE: What does that involve?

PAMELA: Well, it's a detoxifying body scrub followed by lots of lovely body lotion.

CONNIE: That sounds quite diva-rish, but not quite.

PAMELA: Then it sounds like you'll be needing the nutmeg, citrus, ginger, cinnamon and mandarin body mask with a couple of cucumbers for the eyes.

CONNIE: Yes, that sounds more like it.

PAMELA: Well go in the wet room Madge, I mean Connie, and I'll be with you in a moment.

CHRISTINE: But Colin is dying Rose's hair in there.

PAMELA: I think he could do with the excitement.

(EXIT **CONNIE**)

SCENE 11

PAMELA: So, Chris, what do you think of Brutus?

CHRISTINE: He's okay. As I said before, he's just a bit full on. What do you want me to say?

PAMELA: Do you like him?

CHRISTINE: Er...yes. More importantly, do you?

PAMELA: Oh yes.

CHRISTINE: I can see why you were trying to persuade him to get a wax. I'd like to see that chest as smooth as a baby's bottom.

PAMELA: I think I'm changing my mind about that. I quite like the way it greets me before he does.

CHRISTINE:Good, because I don't think there is enough wax in the world to do the job.

PAMELA: Enough about my Sex God. What about your Roger? Come on, tell me while we're alone because we won't be alone for long.

CHRISTINE: There's not much to tell.

PAMELA: Don't be coy.

CHRISTINE: Well, he's nothing like Brutus.

PAMELA: I'm not sure how to take that.

CHRISTINE: He's very romantic.

PAMELA: As is Brutus.

CHRISTINE: Exciting.

PAMELA: As is Brutus.

CHRISTINE: Boyish at times, silly even.

PAMELA: Brutus again.

CHRISTINE: Strong, protective...

PAMELA: Like Brutus.

CHRISTINE: ...but not clingy.

PAMELA: No, neither is Brutus.

CHRISTINE: Well, I may as well tell you.

PAMELA: What?

CHRISTINE: Promise you won't tell anyone.

PAMELA: Go on.

CHRISTINE: I think he's hinting about...well...marriage.

PAMELA: Really? What kind of hints?

CHRISTINE: Like how lovely the engagement rings are in the local jewellers.

PAMELA: That's not a hint. That's a proposal. Anything else?

CHRISTINE: He points out wedding dresses and tells me how lovely I'd look in them.
He also bought some holiday brochures and is showing me the best honeymoon spots.

PAMELA: Hello ? Is anybody home?

CHRISTINE: What?

PAMELA: Wake up and smell the roses. Well, the wedding bouquet at least.

CHRISTINE: If he wants to tell me something, he should just come out with it.

PAMELA: You should marry him. It's not like you don't know what to expect, if you know what I mean.

CHRISTINE: No, I don't know what you mean.

PAMELA: Well, they'll be no nasty surprises on your wedding night. (CHRISTINE LOOKS CONFUSED) Because you'll know what he's like in the bedroom   department.

CHRISTINE: Oh, but we haven't...er...

PAMELA: What?

CHRISTINE: Well we haven't gone down that path yet.

PAMELA: You're kidding me?

CHRISTINE: He's a bit old fashioned that way.

PAMELA: No wonder he wants to get married.

SCENE 12

(ENTER ROSE AND COLIN. ROSE HAS A TOWEL ON HER HEAD,
COVERING HER HAIR)

CHRISTINE: So, you did the deed then.

COLIN: Yes, and I want everyone to be here for the unveiling.

PAMELA: But you scared them all off Colin.

CHRISTINE:Is Connie still in the wet room?

ROSE: Yes. She's taken off all her clothes.

COLIN: Apart from a leotard and the two pointy things.

PAMELA: I'll better go in.

COLIN: No, wait. The unveiling.

CHRISTINE: Oh yes, the unveiling.

COLIN: Take it off Rose.

(ROSE TAKES OFF THE TOWEL. HER HAIR IS BRIGHT GREEN.
EVERYONE GASPS APART FROM ROSE).

CHRISTINE: Oh Colin. What have you done?

COLIN: (TO HIMSELF) Could it have been the chlorine ? Or maybe the
copper deposits?

PAMELA: Let me see Rose. (INSPECTS HER HAIR) It doesn't look like
it's going to fall out at least.

ROSE: What does it look like. Can I see?

CHRISTINE: Brace yourself. (GETS A MIRROR)

ROSE: (PAUSE) Oh.

COLIN: Maybe it was the snail slime ?

ROSE: I like it actually.

PAMELA: Oh Rose, surely not?

ROSE: It's a lovely shade of green.

COLIN: Oh before I forget, I got you some perfume Christine. Don't worry, I didn't invent it.

ROSE: Does Roger know you're getting perfume from strange men ?

PAMELA: Colin's not exactly strange Rose. We've known him for ages.

ROSE: She's engaged isn't she?

CHRISTINE: No. She's not.

PAMELA: Well, not yet.

CHRISTINE: Shush !

PAMELA: Come on Rose, let's try to wash it out.

ROSE: I don't want to wash it out. I like it. It beats those blue rinses. It's very nice Colin. It'll do for the wedding I'm going to next week. (PAUSE) Colin, would you like to come to a wedding with me ?

COLIN: Er...okay.

ROSE: We could have tea and scones afterwards.

(EXIT COLIN AND ROSE)

CHRISTINE: Well, we'd better see to Connie. You can't leave diva's waiting for too long. She'll be freezing her pointy things off.

(EXIT **COLIN**, **ROSE** AND **CHRISTINE**)

SCENE 13

(ENTER SHERRY)

PAMELA: Oh hello, Sherry. You look like the cat who got the cream. What will it be ?

SHERRY: Oh, I only came in for a natter. How's Brutus?

PAMELA: I don't know why people are so interested in my Brutus.

SHERRY: Oh, it's my Brutus now is it?

PAMELA: Sort off. How did your date go last night?

SHERRY: It went very well. The nails snagged the man. That reminds me, is Colin about? I was thinking of buying a few more more bottles.

PAMELA: He's in our bad books. He turned Rose's hair green.

SHERRY: Well, that will be handy if she wants to join one of those punk bands. What about Connie?

PAMELA: She dressed up as Madonna, went into the wet room and never came out.

SHERRY: So, everything's as it should be.

PAMELA: Yes, it's a normal day. So, tell me about the date then. I want all the juicy detail.

SHERRY: Well, you know when I said this new guy acted like a puppy?

PAMELA: Yes?

SHERRY: Well, he's taking it a bit too literally. He followed me into the bedroom again.

PAMELA: Oh yes.

SHERRY: And started sniffing in the corners.

PAMELA: Really?

SHERRY: He cocked his leg against the dressing table...and then...well..

what he did next really shocked me...and I'm not easily shockable.

PAMELA: Tell me.

(ENTER ROGER)

ROGER: Is...er...is Christine about?

PAMELA: She will be somewhere. Tell me.

SHERRY: Well, as you know I'm very broad minded but this...this will

blow your mind...

ROGER: I really need to see her. Christine !

PAMELA: I'll get her in a moment. Please take a seat. Tell me.

SHERRY: Well he... (ENTER **COLIN**)

COLIN: Is Christine about ?

ROGER: Christine ! Christine !

(PAMELA CRIES OUT IN EXASPERATION AND EXITS. ROGER

SITS DOWN)

SCENE 14

SHERRY: Hello.

ROGER: Hello.

SHERRY: Are you okay?

ROGER: Yes.

SHERRY: Only you seem a bit nervous.

ROGER: I'm fine.

SHERRY: Is that sweat on your brow...and lower lip?

ROGER: No, I'm...it's just a bit hot in here isn't it?

SHERRY: Not particularly. (PAUSE) Do you like my nail polish?

(ENTER CHRISTINE AND PAMELA. ENTER CONNIE)

CONNIE: Wow, that was a great massage. Fit for a superstar.

CHRISTINE: Roger.

ROGER: Christine.

PAMELA: If you want a bit of privacy, you can go in the wet room.

ROGER: No. I want everyone to see this.

CHRISTINE: See what?

(ROGER GETS DOWN ON ONE KNEE)

COLIN: Christine. I have some chocolates...

PAMELA: Not now Colin.

ROGER: Christine. (HE TAKES OUT A RING) Will you...could..you... (HE COUGHS) We only met a few months ago but the time I've spend with you has been amazing. I know, it's a bit soon, but I believe in whirlwind romances. I know you do too. I was wondering if you would do me the honour of spending the rest of your life with me. (PAUSE)

CHRISTINE: I..er...

ROGER: I promise you, you won't regret it?

CHRISTINE: Roger, it's...it's so sudden and in front of everyone.

ROGER: I know, I know, you wouldn't believe the courage I've had to find from somewhere to do this.

CHRISTINE: I see.

(PAUSE)

ROGER: Well?

CHRISTINE: I'm sorry. I can't.

(ROGER STANDS UP AND EXITS DESPONTENTLY)

PAMELA: Christine, you said no.

CHRISTINE: I know.

PAMELA: But why?

CHRISTINE: I don't know. He...he caught me off guard, I suppose.

PAMELA: Well, you'll just have to explain when you see him again.

CHRISTINE: No. Don't you see Pamela, it's over. I've just humiliated him. Everything was going so well. He's spoilt it. I've spoilt it.

(EXIT CHRISTINE, CRYING)

PAMELA: Well, don't just stand there gawping everyone. Get back to doing what you were doing before that man proposed to my friend and she turned him down.

SHERRY: We weren't doing anything.

PAMELA: Well...

(ENTER CHRISTINE)

CHRISTINE: I'm sorry that was very unprofessional of me. I should get back to work.

PAMELA: Could everyone please make their way to the refreshment lounge for a moment.

CONNIE: Well, don't just stand there, let's get to it..

(EXIT CONNIE AND COLIN)

PAMELA: What about you Sherry ?

SHERRY: I'm quite comfortable sitting here.

PAMELA: They'll be free tea and coffee.

(EXIT SHERRY) (EXIT PAMELA AND CHRISTINE)

SCENE 15

CHRISTINE: I wasn't aware that we had a refreshment lounge.

PAMELA: We don't. It's just a corridor with a drinks machine.

CHRISTINE: Oh Pam, what have I done ? He was the best thing that ever happened to me.

PAMELA: Well explain to him that you were taken by surprise. He'll understand.

CHRISTINE: No. I've blown it.

PAMELA: Why do you think you turned him down?

CHRISTINE: I froze. I was terrified.

PAMELA: Well, marriage is a big thing, especially to an independent women.

CHRISTINE: Yes. Maybe that was it. I was afraid of losing my independence.

PAMELA: Your sense of identity is already set in stone Chris and you said he wasn't clingy.

CHRISTINE: True. He's not clingy.

PAMELA: I mean, would you say I was independent?

CHRISTINE: Fiercely.

PAMELA: But look at me and Brutus. I'd never be truly independent if I married him. They'll always be three of us in the relationship.

CHRISTINE: Three ?

PAMELA: Me, him and the chest hair. (CHRISTINE LAUGHS) Now, that's better.

CHRISTINE: If he asked me again, I'd say yes like a shot. Although there's not much chance of that.

PAMELA: You never know.

CHRISTINE: I think I'm okay now.

PAMELA: Are you sure ?

CHRISTINE: The show must go on. I'll just go and freshen up.

PAMELA: There couldn't be a better place to do it.

(EXIT CHRISTINE. ENTER ROSE, STILL WITH GREEN HAIR.
ENTER COLIN)

SCENE 16

PAMELA: Colin, I'm in no mood for your silly inventions.

ROSE: That's no way to talk to Colin.

PAMELA: I'm sorry but it's been an exhausting day. Roger came in.

ROSE: Roger ?

PAMELA: Yes and he got down on one knee and proposed to Christine.

ROSE: Really?

PAMELA: Really and she turned him down.

ROSE: What?

PAMELA: And she's very upset.

COLIN: Is she really ? I'm better go and cheer her up.

(ENTER CHRISTINE)

PAMELA: Oh, she's here.

(COLIN COMFORTS CHRISTINE AND GIVES HER THE CHOCOLATES)

ROSE: Why did she turn him down?

PAMELA: She was taken by surprise.

ROSE: That's bad news. That means she's saving herself for someone else.

PAMELA: Who?

ROSE: My Colin.

COLIN: And if you need me for anything Christine. Just let me know.

(EXIT COLIN)

ROSE: Well, I think it's disgusting.

PAMELA: What is.

ROSE: She is.

CHRISTINE: What's that?

ROSE: She's got no shame.

CHRISTINE: Excuse me ? Are you talking to me?

ROSE: She already has a man and now she's trying to take mine.

CHRISTINE: If you've got a problem with me Rose, I'd like you to tell me to my face.

ROSE: Talk to the hand.

CHRISTINE: You treat me like dirt and I've just about had enough of it. I hope your hair stays green forever.

(EXIT CHRISTINE)

ROSE: What's up with her?

PAMELA: She's upset.

ROSE: So she should be.

PAMELA: Rose, she loves Roger. She's not interested in Colin. She only turned him down because she got cold feet. She thinks she's messed things up with him and that he won't want to see her again.

ROSE: If that's the case, we have got to get them back together again. I mean for my sake as well as hers. I can't have Colin moving in on her.

PAMELA: She's vulnerable.

ROSE: And so is he.

PAMELA: Yes, you're right. Well, what can we do? Didn't you say Roger lived next door to Mrs Farley ?

ROSE: Yes I did.

PAMELA: Didn't you say she was Roger's mother?

ROSE: Yes, she is.

PAMELA: Where are you going?

ROSE: I'm going to have a chat with Mrs. Farley.

(EXIT ROSE AND PAMELA)

SCENE 17

(ENTER BRUTUS)

BRUTUS: Pamela? Pamela? My beautiful Pamela. Where are you baby? Do not desert me my sweetness.

(EXIT BRUTUS)

(ENTER ROGER)

ROGER: Hello ? Is anyone there ? Christine? Pamela ? Anyone?

(EXIT ROGER)

(ENTER PAMELA)

PAMELA: I thought I heard someone calling my name. (ENTER ROGER) Roger.

ROGER: Is Christine about?

PAMELA: I don't know where she is.

ROGER: I'm only here because some lady with green hair told my mum that I really must get back with Christine. I didn't think it would be a good idea but my mum's a bit superstitious and took it as an omen. I do miss Christine.

PAMELA: She misses you Roger.

ROGER: Does she?

PAMELA: And she does want to marry you.

ROGER: Does she?

PAMELA: She told me she loves you.

ROGER: Did she really?

PAMELA: Yes, so please stay. Christine should be around here somewhere. She told me that if you proposed to her again, she would say yes.

ROGER: I'm not sure if I could propose to her again. I don't want to make the same mistake twice.

PAMELA: Well, you're going to have to. Now calm yourself. You're shaking.

ROGER: I'm a bag of nerves.

PAMELA: I know what might calm you down.

ROGER: Oh?

PAMELA: A body mask. You've had one before remember ?

ROGER: Oh yes.

PAMELA: Didn't that relax you then?

ROGER: Yes, as a matter of fact.

PAMELA: I could give you a very refreshing apricot and mango wrap and after the stimulation of the exfoliation, I'll slather the body with a very soothing, calming lubricant.

ROGER: It's not a body oil is it? I mean I don't like greasy oils.

PAMELA: Rest assured it's not a body oil.

ROGER: Oh, that's okay then.

PAMELA: It's a lotion.

(EXIT PAMELA AND ROGER)

SCENE 18

(ENTER CHRISTINE, SHERRY, CONNIE AND ROSE)

ROSE: A manicure for me.

CONNIE: A facial please.

SHERRY: I would like a pedicure. Chameleon is progressing to the feet, or rather the new boyfriend is.

CHRISTINE: But I can't right now. I don't know where Pamela is. Can you please step into the refreshment lounge for a little while.

CONNIE: But I have no time for refreshment. I need to work tirelessly for all the poor children of the earth.

CHRISTINE: Er...

CONNIE: I didn't have children of my own so that I would have the time and energy to mother the whole world.

SHERRY: Have you guessed yet?

(PAUSE)

CONNIE: It is God's will.

CHRISTINE: Mother Theresa, will you please lead these lost souls into the refreshment lounge.

(EXIT CONNIE, SHERRY AND ROSE)

(ENTER ROGER AND PAMELA)

CHRISTINE: Oh Pamela, there you are. Oh Roger. What are you doing here?

ROGER: I just had a body mask followed by a very relaxing massage.

CHRISTINE: You gave my Roger a massage?

PAMELA: It's not like it hasn't happened before. As you know the Salt

Glow stimulates the body and the massage is essential for calming the body.

(ENTER DEVIANT)

DEVIANT: Can I have the full body massage please?

PAMELA: We told you, we don't do massages.

DEVIANT: Well in that case, I'll just have a short back and sides.

PAMELA: I'll be with you in a moment. Could you please step into the refreshment lounge. (EXIT DEVIANT)

In fact, let's all step into the refreshment lounge.

CHRISTINE: Wait. I'm not finished with you yet.

(EXIT PAMELA AND ROGER)

SCENE 19

(ENTER BRUTUS)

BRUTUS: Where is Pamela?

CHRISTINE: I'll tell you where Pamela is...actually...come to think of it...I haven't seen her for a while. I believe she's very busy. Is there anything I can do for you?

BRUTUS: I need to see my Pamela. I haven't seen her since last night and I'm missing her.

CHRISTINE: Really?

BRUTUS: And I'm pining for her.

CHRISTINE: As I say, she's busy at the moment, busy being a two faced cow.

BRUTUS: Sorry?

CHRISTINE: Never mind. Let's go into the wet room Brutus.

BRUTUS: Wet room ? Sounds sexy.

CHRISTINE: It will be when I've finished with you.

(EXIT CHRISTINE. EXIT BRUTUS)

(ENTER SHERRY, CONNIE, DEVIANT, ROSE AND PAMELA)

PAMELA: Where are you all going ? I told you to wait in the refreshment lounge.

DEVIANT: It's just a corridor with a drinks machine.

PAMELA: Okay, you'd better all come back in then. Everyone just pile in. The more the merrier. Well come on, you'd better all sit down.

SHERRY: I want a pedicure remember.

DEVIANT: And I'm having a short back and sides.

ROSE: I want a manicure with green nail polish to match my hair

(BRUTUS SCREAMS BACKSTAGE)

CONNIE: And I don't need anything. I'm a giver, not a taker. Well actually it is my birthday. I might have a wax.

PAMELA: Of course. What part of the body would you like waxed?

CONNIE: I don't know. Do you have a price list?

(BRUTUS SCREAMS AGAIN BACKSTAGE)

PAMELA: Okay, for half a leg it's £20.

CONNIE: That's quite reasonable.

PAMELA: For three quarters of a leg it's £29.

CONNIE: Mmmm, go on.

PAMELA: For a full leg it's £35.

CONNIE: Starting to get a bit steep.

PAMELA: Well the more we defuzz, the pricier it gets.

(BRUTUS SCREAMS AGAIN)

For a regular bikini it's £17.

For a Brazilian landing strip it's £27.

And for a Hollywood All Off...

CONNIE: A what?

PAMELA: A Hollywood All Off, it's £37. (BRUTUS SCREAMS AGAIN)

So, what do you fancy?

CONNIE: I think I've changed my mind.

(ENTER CHRISTINE)

CHRISTINE: Come on Brutus. Out you come.

BRUTUS: But...but...I can't.

CHRISTINE: Yes, you can. Don't be a wimp.

BRUTUS: But I feel naked.

CHRISTINE: You'll get used to it. I promise.

(ENTER BRUTUS MINUS CHEST HAIR)

PAMELA: What have you done? Oh Brutus, where's your rug ?

BRUTUS: She...she took it off and it hurt. It really hurt.

PAMELA: Christine, how could you?

CHRISTINE: Well, you body masked my Roger twice and massaged him countless times. You've seen him naked more times than I have.

PAMELA: Well, that wouldn't be difficult would it, but yes, you have a point, but I only did it to calm him down so he could..he could...

CHRISTINE: Could what?

PAMELA: You'll see.

BRUTUS: I'm cold.

PAMELA: Oh my poor lamb. Come here.

CHRISTINE: He's much better post wax. You'll thank me for it, you'll see.

SHERRY: Let's have a look Brutus. Oh yes, smooth as a baby's bottom.

CONNIE: I shall minister to those in need. Come here **BRUTUS.**

PAMELA: Stay were you are Connie. Come here Brutus. (HUGS BRUTUS) There, there, all warm now.

SCENE 20

(ENTER ROGER)

ROGER: Christine

CHRISTINE: Roger

(ROGER GETS DOWN ON ONE KNEE)

ROGER: Christine?

CHRISTINE: Yes ?

(ENTER COLIN)

COLIN: I've got it !

(EVERYONE GROANS)

PAMELA: Not now Colin.

ROSE: Yes, for once, not now Colin.

COLIN: No. I've really got it this time. It really works this time. No more botox pillow cheeks, no more frozen face, no more bee sting lip. Just a beautiful woman look. I'll be a millionaire, a billionaire.

PAMELA: The day you invent an actual wonder cream, one that makes wrinkles disappear and reverses ageing, is the day I'll appear in the buff on top of Blackpool Tower.

ROSE: I'll hold you to that.

SHERRY: We're not interested any more Colin.

PAMELA: You've cried wolf too many times.

CONNIE: We forgive you Colin.

PAMELA: No, we don't. We're judging you on your past mistakes I'm afraid.

ROSE: I'll try it Colin.

PAMELA: No, you won't. We need to hear Christine's answer.

SHERRY: Off you go Colin.

COLIN: But I have flowers. (CHRISTINE SIGHS AND GOES TO GET THE FLOWERS BUT HE HANDS THEM TO ROSE) How about some lunch?

ROSE: Sounds wonderful.

(EXIT COLIN AND ROSE)

PAMELA: Well come on Roger, get your finger out, or rather hers, put a ring on it.

SHERRY: He must be getting terrible cramp down there.

CONNIE: Here let me help you.

PAMELA: Stay were you are Connie.

ROGER: Oh er...ahem...Christine. Will you marry me?

(PAUSE)

CHRISTINE: Yes ! Yes, Roger, I will marry you.

(CHRISTINE AND ROGER HUG)

PAMELA: At last. Well come on let's go and celebrate.

(EXIT PAMELA, CHRISTINE, ROGER, SHERRY, CONNIE, DEVIANT AND BRUTUS)

SCENE 21

(ENTER COLIN WITH ROSE ON HIS ARM)

ROSE: Read it out loud Colin. I want the whole world to hear this.

COLIN: (READS FROM NEWSPAPER) Local man Colin Huxley, has invented a new skin emollient, which is being hailed as a wonder cream. The face lotion visibly smooths away wrinkles and reverses the ageing process of the skin. A leading global cosmetics company has snapped up his idea and is set to make Mr. Huxley a multi millionaire.

ROSE: Billionaire Colin.

COLIN: Yes Rose. Shall we step onto the yacht? The champagne will be chilled by now.

ROSE: Wait. There's one more thing.

(ENTER PAMELA AND CHRISTINE)

COLIN: Pamela, why are you in a robe?

ROSE: Surely you haven't forgotten. She said the day you invent a wonder cream is the day she would appear in the buff on top of...

COLIN: Yes, I remember. Are you really going to make her do it?

(ENTER SHERRY, CONNIE, DEVIANT, CHRISTINE, ROGER AND BRUTUS)

PAMELA: This lot won't let me forget either. They missed out on a free sample of wonder cream remember.

COLIN: I think I have a little to spare. It's only one thousand pound per jar at the moment, although the price is set to rise.

CHRISTINE: Who are you today Connie ?

CONNIE: Oh, I'm just me today.

CHRISTINE: That's the best person you've been all week.

SHERRY: Yes, the true you. You should just be yourself from now on.

CONNIE: I feel so exposed.

CHRISTINE: Don't worry, you're not alone. Pamela, is going to expose herself today.

PAMELA: Oh well, Blackpool tower here I come.

BRUTUS: You will not need Blackpool lights. You will light up all of Blackpool.

ROGER: Well, you'll certainly draw the crowds.

COLIN: You're being very brave. Actually, I have a complimentary jar of my miracle cream right here. You can have it. (GIVES IT TO PAMELA)

CHRISTINE: You know, it is rather warm out today. I might join you.

PAMELA: Keep your hands off. (HOLDS THE CREAM CLOSE TO HER CHEST. A TUG OF WAR WITH CHRISTINE ENSUES)

(EXIT EVERYONE)

(AFTER THE CAST RETURN FOR THEIR BOW AND THE CURTAINS CLOSE, PAMELA LETS THE BATHROBE DROP OUTSIDE THE CURTAINS)

THE END